GAYBCs

A QUEER ALPHABET

rae congdon

GREYSTONE BOOKS

Vancouver/Berkeley

Found this book tucked
away on a shelf and decided
to make some changes...

Just like the original words,
these new ones should be
part of our basic vocabulary
so they can be properly
understood and embraced.

Someone who supports LGBTQ+ people and causes

~~Apple~~ ALLY

Attracted to more
than one gender

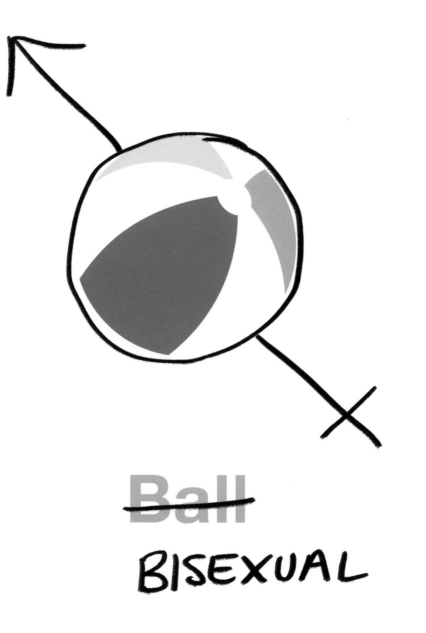

~~Ball~~

BISEXUAL

Describes someone who
identifies with their
gender assigned at birth

~~Chick~~

CISGENDER

Subverting gender through art and performance

~~Door~~ DRAG

Having the same status, rights, and opportunities regardless of difference

Eye
EQUALITY

An identity for an LGBTQ+ person who acts or presents in a feminine manner

Flower

FEMME

Attracted to the
same sex

Gay

The worldview that promotes being straight as the norm.
See : every fairy tale ever

~~Hat~~

HETERONORMATIVE

People born with sex characteristics that don't fit the typical male or female constructs

No time for negative!
Live and let live

Good
Apple

JUDGMENT-
FREE

~~Juice~~

(Not your basic)
personal sexual taste

Kiss ~~Kiss~~

KINK

A woman attracted
to other women

~~Ladybug~~
LESBIAN

A gender-neutral alternative to Mr. and Mrs. If it feels right for you, go with it!

Mx.

~~Mail~~

Any gender identity that isn't exclusively man or woman, like genderfluid, 2-spirit, and agender

01234...

NON-BINARY

Numbers

Being open about your
gender and/or sexuality

Preconceived opinion
that isn't based on actual
reason or experience

Originally a slur, now reclaimed by many. Anyone in the LGBTQ+ community can choose to identify as queer.

Queen

Designed in 1978 by
Gilbert Baker. The original
flag had 8 colors, each
with their own meaning

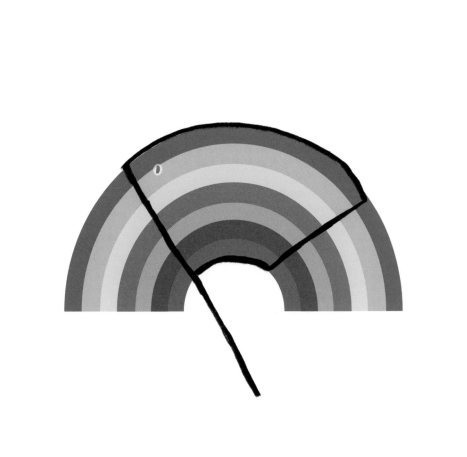

Rainbow

FLAG

How we express sexual
feelings, desires, and behavior

SEXUALITY

Describes someone who identifies with a gender different than the one assigned at birth

~~Tie~~

TRANSGENDER

Things that aren't gender specific. Clothes are clothes - anything goes

Umbrella

UNISEX

Throwing shade through
dance - originated with
Black and Latinx drag
queens in the NYC
ballroom scene

~~Visor~~

VOGUING

Something bold
Something new
Something real
Something true

Wedding

Hugs + kisses

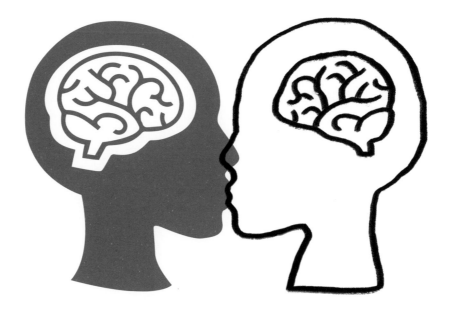

xoxo

~~X-ray~~

LGBTQ+ Kids -
Support them
Respect them
Be their friend

~~Yellow~~

YOUTH

Ze and they are some gender-neutral alternatives to he and she.

To each their own!

Zebra

18 19 20 21 22   5 4 3 2 1

Greystone Books Ltd.
greystonebooks.com

Cataloguing data available from Library and Archives Canada
ISBN 978-1-77164-394-8(cloth)
ISBN 978-1-77164-395-5 (epub)

Editing by Paula Ayer
Sensitivity reading by Vivek Shraya
Jacket and interior design by Rae Congdon
Printed and bound in China on ancient-forest-friendly paper by 1010 Printing Asia Ltd.

We gratefully acknowledge the support of the Canada Council for the Arts, the British Columbia Arts Council, the Province of British Columbia through the Book Publishing Tax Credit, and the Government of Canada for our publishing activities.

Canada

 Canada Council   Conseil des arts
for the Arts   du Canada

 BRITISH COLUMBIA   BRITISH COLUMBIA ARTS COUNCIL
An agency of the Province of British Columbia

RAINBOW
RAILROAD

A portion of the proceeds from *GAYBCs* will be donated to Rainbow Railroad, a registered charitable organization based in Toronto, Canada. Rainbow Railroad provides support to LGBTQI individuals around the world who are seeking a safe haven from state-sponsored or enabled violence.

Acknowledgments

A huge thank you to everyone at Greystone Books, specifically Rob Sanders for his interest and enthusiasm and my editor Paula Ayer for her amazing work.

This book may not have caught the eye of Liz Culotti and my incredible agent Jackie Kaiser of Westwood Creative Artists if the Adobe Design Achievement Awards hadn't recognized it in 2016, so thank you to the ADAA team and the judging panel.

Vivek Shraya, David Ayllon, and Topher Cusumano – I can't thank you enough for your feedback and ideas. To my friends and family, thank you for your support and inspiration.

About the Author

Rae Congdon is an award-winning Canadian graphic designer and a graduate of Seton Hall University, where she studied graphic and interactive design with a minor in fine arts. *GAYBCs*, her first book, was awarded an Adobe Design Achievement Award in the Social Impact category. Rae lives in Montreal, Quebec.